PROJECT PUFFIN

A National Audubon Society Book

PROJECT PUFFIN:

BY Stephen W. Kress AS TOLD TO Pete Salmansohn

How We Brought Puffins Back to Egg Rock

Tilbury House, Publishers • Gardiner, Maine

A National  Audubon Society Book

Preface

Some people call them clowns of the sea. Others know them as comical little sea parrots. But whatever you call them, puffins are adorable! With those large, colorful beaks, their upright posture, and their dark, soulful eyes, it's easy to see why puffins are popular all over the world.

Many people think puffins are two or three feet tall, but they are really only about the height of a jug of milk—about ten inches. And they weigh a little bit more than a can of soda—about one pound.

When they fly, they look like a black and white football with wings beating so fast all you can see is a quickly moving blur. Some folks even say a puffin in the air flies like a big bumblebee. And they beat those wings fast—about 300 to 400 times per minute!

But many years ago, almost all the puffins along the Maine Coast had been killed. This book tells the exciting and true story of how one man with a dream set out to accomplish something no one had ever done before— bring the puffins back!

—Pete Salmansohn

When I take my boat out to Eastern Egg Rock now, I remember my first trip to this tiny island off the coast of Maine. It was a cloudy day in June of 1969, and as my boat circled the island I could see only gulls and a few eider ducks. There were no puffins anywhere. From my reading, I knew that it had been almost 100 years since puffins were last seen here. I looked at the quiet ocean around me, and I felt sad.

In my mind, however, I could see the chunky little puffins whizzing through the air. I could picture their stubby black wings beating quickly, and their snowy white chests looking bright against the sky. If puffins once lived here, why did they leave? Was it possible they might come back again? I began thinking how, as a wildlife scientist, I might help to bring puffins back to Eastern Egg Rock.

(far left) Audubon wildlife scientist Steve Kress
(above) Puffins once nested under these boulders. Would these places be used again?

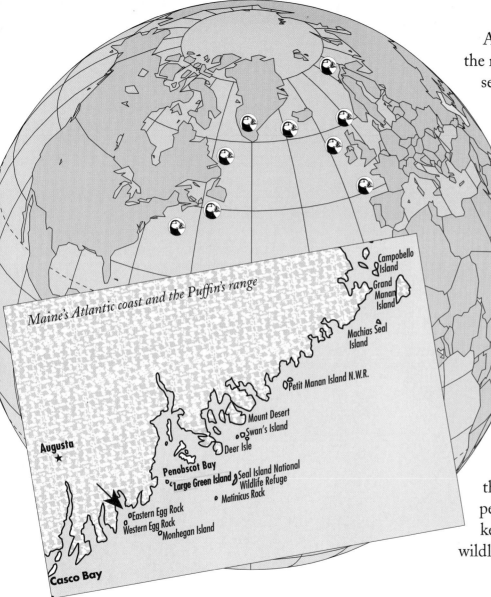

Maine's Atlantic coast and the Puffin's range

Campobello Island

Grand Manan Island

Machias Seal Island

Petit Manan Island N.W.R.

Mount Desert

Swan's Island

Deer Isle

Penobscot Bay

Large Green Island

Seal Island National Wildlife Refuge

Matinicus Rock

Augusta

Eastern Egg Rock

Western Egg Rock

Monhegan Island

Casco Bay

As I turned my boat towards home, I thought about the reasons why puffins had disappeared. Pioneers who settled here in the 1600s began killing seabirds for food. As more settlers came to New England during the next few centuries, more birds were shot not only for their meat, but also for their feathers. Some feathers were used to stuff pillows and mattresses. And some decorated women's hats.

But before those early settlers came to New England, puffins nested on at least six islands along the Maine coast—Eastern Egg Rock, Western Egg Rock, Large Green Island, Matinicus Rock, Seal Island, and Machias Seal Island.

By 1901, after centuries of hunting, there remained only one pair of puffins south of the Canadian border. That pair lived on Matinicus Rock, a lonely outpost twenty-two miles from the Maine shoreline, in Penobscot Bay. All the other puffins had been killed. But in that same year, a group of scientists and concerned people hired the Matinicus Rock lighthouse keeper to keep the gunners away. He was one of America's first wildlife wardens.

Typical hat with seabird wings, 1880s.

With Matinicus Rock under protection from hunting, puffins began to come back. Over the years, new lighthouse keepers and wardens from the National Audubon Society took over their protection. In 1918, Congress passed a law called the Migratory Bird Treaty Act, which made it illegal to kill most kinds of wild birds. Now there are about 150 pairs of puffins who call Matinicus Rock their home. This proves to me that if people take the time to care and act, seabird colonies can be restored.

Puffins at the Matinicus Rock lighthouse.

Great Black-backed Gulls

But puffins never came back to Eastern Egg Rock and three other islands they used to call home. Why? Probably because large and hungry gulls had taken over. There is now more food for the gulls—garbage, factory wastes, and dead fish and fish parts cast off boats—and gull populations have greatly increased. Not only can they eat these food wastes that other birds such as puffins and terns don't use, but they also raise two or three chicks a year. A puffin has only one chick each breeding season.

Gulls will eat a puffin's egg if they can find one, as

Great Cormorant

well as puffin chicks and adults! Because of the aggressive gulls, puffins never had a chance to return home. If one even visited an island where its ancestors used to

Common Eider

nest, it would be chased away by the gulls. Puffins are actually rather timid birds—certainly no match for a hungry gull.

As I visited a number of Maine Islands, I was delighted to see how many of them were alive with birdlife. Eider ducks, cormorants, and Black Guillemots had all made a comeback since the earlier days of feather hunting. And there were lots of gulls wherever I looked. But the islands seemed incomplete without puffins and terns. I felt a deep sense of loss.

Leach's Storm-Petrel

Black Guillemot

I began talking with many people who had spent their lives studying puffins and other seabirds. I shared with them my hope of bringing puffins back to Eastern Egg Rock. They all told me nothing like that had ever been done before. Some even said it was impossible, but others offered encouragement and told me that if I wanted to make my dream come true, I should learn as much as I could about how puffins live.

Puffins rest and nest on land.

I learned that puffins are truly birds of the open ocean and spend most of their lives far from the sight of land. In fact, a puffin is very much at home floating and paddling about on the water's surface. They are excellent divers and are known to swim to depths of more than 100 feet in search of fish to eat. While some seabirds kick their feet for underwater swimming, puffins beat their wings, as if they're flying. They use their webbed feet as rudders, for steering. I've watched as they stay under for more than thirty seconds.

How does a puffin manage to catch and hold all those fish in its beak? Scientists believe that the puffin uses its raspy tongue to push the fish against tiny backward-pointing barbs on the roof of the mouth. Each time another fish is caught, the tongue pushes and holds it up with the others. It's often difficult to count, but I've seen more than a dozen small fish in a puffin's beak at one time. The record load is sixty-two!

The puffin's beak and mouthparts are made to grasp slippery fish.

A puffin lays just one egg per breeding season.

If puffins survive their winter at sea, they will return to their nesting island for one reason—to raise a chick. A female puffin lays its single egg in a rocky crevice or at the end of a long, earthen tunnel. I've seen burrows that were eight feet long! One explanation for the use of underground chambers is that it's a good way to hide from gulls.

When puffins dig their burrows in soil, they use their strong beaks and sharp toenails. Parent puffins incubate the egg for a long time: forty-two days or more.

Once the chick hatches, it must be kept warm by its parents for several days. It sits under its mother's or father's wing, nestling close to the body. This is known as brooding. Soon, the chick's own body stays warm by itself. Then the parents spend most of their time out at sea, fishing for herring, hake, and other food to bring back for their chick. When the adult comes in with a load of fish, it usually drops the fish in the burrow and then quickly leaves, either to rest on the rocks or go out fishing again. The chick spends most of its time alone, underground.

For about six more weeks the hungry chick eats twenty to twenty-five fish a day. It uses a separate little toilet area back in the burrow for the first few weeks of its life. As it

gets older, it squirts along the walls of the burrow and then eventually points its rear end out the burrow entrance—first peering outside to see if any gulls are lurking. By staying clean, the chick keeps its feathers from getting soiled, and they remain water-proof for a future life on the ocean.

A very young chick, about a week old.

The chick also comes out of its burrow at night to exercise its wings. It does this because it is getting ready to fledge—to take flight and go to sea. As the chick's fledging night approaches, the chick paces back and forth in its burrow.

One night in August, the chick is ready. It comes out of its burrow and hops down to the sea. Then it jumps into the water and paddles off without its parents. By early the next morning, the fledgling is already far from land, away from predatory gulls. And, as surprising as this may sound, the little puffin does not come back to land for two or three years. It lives on the ocean during this entire time.

Of course, not all young puffins survive the dangers of life alone, at sea. Only about three or four out of every ten birds ever grow up to have chicks of their own. But a healthy puffin can live to be twenty-five years old.

Humans haven't figured out how puffins find their way back to their nesting island. Perhaps they use the stars, sense a magnetic tug, or hear the sounds of the surf. Maybe the island has its own unique smell. Puffins might take these clues to create a mental map, which they use several years later when it's time to return.

If puffins were ever to live on Eastern Egg Rock again, I knew we would have to find a large colony where there were enough of them to move some to Maine.

A six-week-old puffin.

If we brought those chicks to Eastern Egg Rock, maybe they would adopt it as their new home and come back to nest there when they were older. That was my hope. I had no way of knowing if this plan would work. No one had ever tried to start a puffin colony before. I was very nervous. What if the chicks died? What if they were never seen again? It was very risky. But I felt it was the only way we would ever see puffins return to Eastern Egg Rock.

Scientists from the Canadian Wildlife Service agreed to help me with my plan, and in July of 1973 I flew to Newfoundland. I was taken out by boat to the largest puffin colony in North America—Great Island. Here more than 300,000 puffins live in one place. I was amazed at what I saw. Puffins were flying off, and puffins were landing. They were circling overhead by the hundreds, landing with beaks stuffed full of fish. Puffins were everywhere! And the grassy slopes were filled with thousands of burrows the puffins had dug as their nesting places.

Great Island is a perfect place for a colony of puffins. It's close to the Grand Banks, a rich fishing area where seabirds of all types can catch herring, capelin, and other food. It has steep, grassy slopes that are ideal for burrow-building. And it's far enough from shore so there are no mammal predators present, such as skunks, racoons, or rats. The island is now protected as a seabird nesting sanctuary, and the birds are thriving. The Canadian scientists and I believed there were enough puffins on Great Island so we could take some back to Maine without doing harm to this colony.

There were puffins everywhere on Great Island. The hillsides had thousands of burrows and plenty of chicks.

My assistants and I rolled up our sleeves and stuck our arms into the long soil burrows. Sometimes our fingers were nipped by an adult puffin who was inside. That was painful! Sometimes the burrow was empty. But often we were able to find a chick who was just about the right size and age for our experiment.

I imagined the parent birds would probably be startled at first to find their chick was gone, but I knew they'd come back the next year to lay another egg.

We were looking for chicks that were ten to fourteen days old, because that meant they would live on Eastern Egg Rock for a full month before fledging. Hopefully, the chicks would eventually learn that Maine was their home, not Newfoundland.

We carefully placed each chick into a soup can we had nailed inside a wooden box. In 1973, we began with just six baby puffins. The next year we took 54 chicks, and then we increased to about 100 chicks per summer until 1981. By then we had brought 954 downy fuzzballs south to Maine, probably the only time "suitcases" have ever been filled with baby puffins.

The chicks traveled in soup cans, nailed inside a wooden box.

Because puffin chicks live alone in underground burrows, we designed carrying cases with an individual, dark compartment for each chick.

We flew the puffin chicks back to Maine the same day we gathered them. Audubon warden Joe Johansen immediately took us and the cases of baby puffins out to Eastern Egg Rock in a large powerboat. The chicks were quickly taken to individual burrows built of grass and sod, and carefully placed inside. We also had a hundred pounds of fish to feed our new residents. As you might imagine, we were exhausted, but were very excited to finally have the chicks in their new homes.

We treated the chicks like honored guests. Each

This is how we snuck a vitamin into dinner.

Each puffin chick was carefully placed in its own burrow. We numbered the burrows and kept track of each chick.

morning and afternoon a team member put fish at the front of the burrows for the puffins to eat. We even put a vitamin pill into one of the fish every other day so our puffins would be strong.

Whenever we spent time near the burrows we spoke in hushed voices. We also avoided handling the chicks until they were old enough to band. By doing so, I believed we were reducing the human impact and giving them a better chance to survive in the wild.

The chicks were given fish every morning and afternoon and they gobbled them up.

To make sure we knew each and every puffin, we put a colored and numbered plastic band on one leg, and a shiny metal band on the other. Each year we used a different color. This doesn't hurt the birds at all. There's always room for the band to move up and down on the leg. At five weeks old, a puffin's leg is nearly as big as it's going to be.

Before we knew it a few weeks had gone by, it was August, and the chicks were ready to leave. At night we hid behind rocks and watched. Sometimes it was so dark we couldn't see anything. But on some nights, when the moon was out, we could see chicks stumbling their way down to the ocean. As I watched, one bird reached the water's edge and paddled off. I wondered whether we would ever see that puffin again. I thought about all the bad things that could happen, like meeting a shark or swimming into an oil spill or getting tangled in a fishing net. And I also wondered if the chick would find its way back to Eastern Egg Rock. Would it go to Newfoundland where it hatched? I stopped worrying and wished the young puffin, who had now disappeared on the ocean's surface, goodbye and good luck.

(left) We carefully placed identification bands on each puffin's legs.
(right) A young puffin leaves its burrow one night in August and finds its way down to the ocean in the dark of night.

If the young puffins survived their two or three years on the sea and came back to Eastern Egg Rock, I knew we'd have to do something about the gulls. I certainly didn't want to see our returning birds eaten or scared away by the Herring Gulls and Great Black-backed Gulls that nested on the island. I decided to ask the United States Fish and Wildlife Service for their help, because they are in charge of laws affecting America's birds. Biologists from the Service took on the job of preventing gulls from nesting on Eastern Egg Rock. I struggled with this difficult decision because I knew it would bring great disturbances to the gull colony, but I realized that the Puffin Project could not succeed without taking direct action.

We painted dozens of puffin decoys. Would they fool you?

I wondered how Eastern Egg Rock would look to puffins who might be returning. Would it look lonely? Would they be afraid to stay if they didn't see other puffins? That's when I came up with the idea of using decoys. Maybe puffins could be tricked into thinking there were lots of other puffins already there. During the winter we had dozens of decoys carved from wood on a special carving machine, and then we painted them. The following summer we set our new decoys on steel posts and cemented them to the rocks. Then we waited. . . .

Four years after we began our project, the first puffin came back. It was a day I will never forget. I was looking over to the large rock where we had set three decoys. Now, however, there were four puffins, and one was moving! I saw its white-colored leg band and knew it was one of our 1975 transplants. That meant it was a two-year-old bird. Can you imagine my excitement? My dream was coming true!

During the next few years, more and more puffins came back to Eastern Egg Rock. Through our telescopes we could see the colors of their bands and could read their numbers. We never did see any birds, however, from our 1973 and 1974 transplant operation. I wasn't too surprised at that, because we were just beginning to move and raise puffins and were sure to make some mistakes. We never did know how many puffins would return or which transplant years would be most successful. It took many long hours of watching to see which birds showed up.

I was very interested to find out that a few of the 1975 chicks were seen by our wardens on Matinicus Rock, about thirty-two miles away. This meant our puffins were visiting other puffin colonies and might lure some of those birds back to Eastern Egg Rock. That was one way our colony would grow.

My hope of restoring puffins seemed to be coming true. But we were still waiting for the first eggs and chicks.

Three decoys and a puffin. Which is which?

On July 4, 1981, Audubon scientist Evie Weinstein saw an adult puffin flying over the island with fish in its bill. Later that day I saw a puffin, also carrying fish, fly to the rocks and slip into a crevice. A few seconds later it came out without the fish! That meant only one thing—under the boulders a hungry newborn chick was waiting for food.

We shouted with joy! The experiment was a success. Eight years of hard work

When we saw a puffin carrying fish, we knew there was a chick waiting in a burrow.

had paid off. Puffins were finally nesting again on Eastern Egg Rock for the first time in 100 years.

During the next week, we saw even more puffins bring in fish. Sitting inside our observation blinds, we carefully watched the birds so we knew which burrow

We watched each puffin pair carefully and numbered the new burrows.

each was going to. We could see their leg band colors and numbers, and we also kept track of their burrows by painting numbers on the rocks and on sticks.

The first breeding puffins were mainly four-year-old birds. This was surprising because most puffins don't breed until they are five or six. I guessed that because they didn't have competition from an already established group of older puffins, they moved right in. During that first year of nesting—1981—we counted five active nests.

But where were the older birds? Some showed up eventually, and some were seen at other puffin colonies in the Gulf of Maine. And some were never seen at all.

An important part of our experiment was keeping accurate records. We wanted to know exactly which puffins came back, how long they stayed, and with whom they may have been breeding. We noted the weather conditions each day. Did wind direction or other things make a difference in how often we saw puffins? We also wanted to see what kind of fish they were bringing in to the chicks, and how often they made deliveries. You can probably imagine how much time and patience this took. But with the information in our notebooks, we could share our findings with other scientists around the world.

Yes, there were many instances when it was difficult, like trying to read tiny leg band numbers from a distance, or sitting in a cramped observation blind for hours. But sometimes the puffins came as close as six feet to our blinds. That was exciting!

We kept careful records for each bird.

DATE ALL BANDS ON	WING CHORD AT COLLECTION	WING CHORD AT BANDING	BANDS — YELLOW PLASTIC LEFT	BANDS — RIGHT	COMMENTS	WEIGHT AT COLLECTION	WEIGHT AT BANDING
							323
							356
							333
							345
8/1		116	201-201	MONEL 01	ALL BANDS ON 8/1		283
8/2		118	202-202	MONEL 02	ALL BANDS ON 8/2		360
8/1		112	203-203	MONEL 03	ALL BANDS ON 8/1		328
8/1		118	204-204	MONEL 04	ALL BANDS ON 8/1		344
8/1		117	205-205	MONEL 05	ALL BANDS ON 8/1		335
8/1		114	206-206	MONEL 06	ALL BANDS ON 8/1		390
8/1		114	207-207	MONEL 07	ALL BANDS ON 8/1		344
8/1		118	208-208	MONEL 08	ALL BANDS ON 8/1		360
8/1		116	209-209	MONEL 09	ALL BANDS ON 8/1		365
8/1		116	210-210	MONEL 10	ALL BANDS ON 8/1		316
8/1		115	211-211	MONEL 11	ALL BANDS ON 7/31		337
8/1		113	212-212	MONEL 12	ALL BANDS ON 7/31		345
7/31		119	213-213	MONEL 13	ALL BANDS ON 7/31		331
7/31		116	214-214	MONEL 14	ALL BANDS ON 7/31		302
7/31		118	215-215	MONEL 15	ALL BANDS ON 7/31		340
7/31		117	216-216	MONEL 16	ALL BANDS ON 8/1		356
7/31		119	217-217	MONEL 17	ALL BANDS ON 8/1		323
8/1		114	218-218	MONEL 18	ALL BANDS ON 8/1		343
8/1		117	219-219	MONEL 19	ALL BANDS ON 8/1	LICE		37?
8/1		120	220-220	MONEL 20	ALL BANDS ON 8/1		344
8/1		119	221-221	MONEL 21	ALL BANDS ON 8/1		341
8/1		117	222-222	MONEL 22	ALL BANDS ON 7/31	
8/1		121	223-223	MONEL 23	ALL BANDS ON 7/31	
7/31		121	224-224	MONEL 24		
7/31		47	225-225	MONEL 25		

One especially interesting story we've followed over the years is that of En. (engraved band) #25. He came to Eastern Egg Rock in 1979 as a chick and over the years has had three mates. Two died, and one left him for another partner. In 1990 En25 was single again, but the following year, in 1991, he found his fourth mate, a female wearing band U04 (a white band with the number 04). She had mated with Bicolor 12 (he wore a two-color band) during 1989 and 1990, but that bird never returned in 1991. En25 moved out of a burrow he'd been in for several years and joined U04 in her nearby rock crevice. Together they've raised chicks each year since then—a true puffin success story.

Since 1981, the colony has grown. There are now about nineteen pairs of puffins nesting on Eastern Egg Rock. When the birds aren't busy catching fish, they like to get together on the rocks and socialize. From the blind I can sometimes see male and female puffins rubbing their beaks together in a display of affection known as "billing."

Once in a while one puffin may fly in or walk too close to one another. The first bird may hold its bill open, hoping to scare the other bird away. This is called "gaping." The second puffin may open its bill, too. Most of the time one bird flies away or scoots off, but sometimes they lock beaks and begin a struggle that may lead to both birds tumbling off the rocks.

With puffins breeding on Eastern Egg Rock, I wondered if we could start a second colony on Seal Island, in nearby Penobscot Bay. Seal Island is a National Wildlife Refuge. It's 100 acres in size—about 14 times bigger than Eastern Egg Rock. Twenty miles out to sea from Rockland, Maine, it was once Maine's largest puffin colony, but it was also raided many times by hunters, until the last puffins disappeared in the 1880s.

Seal Island was also used by the U.S. Navy during the 1940s and 1950s as a bombing target. Before we were allowed to start the project, the Navy searched for unexploded bombs.

In 1984 the island was considered safe, and we began bringing the first chicks down from Newfoundland. We reared up to 200 chicks at a time, using techniques developed at Egg Rock. Then we waited to see if the puffins would come back to breed. In July of 1992, seven pairs of puffins nested. Since then, each year has seen more puffins breeding. In 1996 we counted forty active burrows! But puffins aren't the only part of the story.

Seal Island is about 100 acres in size — much larger than Egg Rock. It would take you two hours to walk from one end to the other.

erns, a different species of seabird, were also once hunted for their beautiful feathers, and their numbers had fallen over the years. I was very interested in seeing if we could bring them back to some of their old nesting islands, too. After Eastern Egg Rock and Seal Island were safe from hungry gulls, our team set out tern decoys in grassy areas. We played tape recordings of tern colony sounds and set the speakers near the decoys.

Within a few hours of beginning our experiment, terns started landing. This showed me that they were desperate to find a safe place, away from the gulls. During those first few summers, terns visited our islands in greater and greater numbers, but none laid eggs. Finally the day arrived when terns started breeding on the islands. That was a few years ago. If you go out to Seal Island or Eastern Egg Rock now, you will see thousands of terns. In addition to their great beauty, they are fierce defenders of their colony and will successfully drive gulls, crows, and ravens away from their nests. This helps protect the puffin colony.

When the terns leave their nesting islands in August, I'm always amazed to think that one species—the Arctic Tern—will fly all the way to Antarctica. In May the same birds will, hopefully, return to the coast of Maine. It's a round trip of 15,000 to 20,000 miles.

A Common Tern with a decoy.

An endangered Roseate Tern.

A Common Tern with chicks.

Steve Kress holds an endangered Dark-rumped Petrel chick in the Galapagos Islands.

Even though Project Puffin has faced many serious challenges over the years, I've never given up on my dream. I've learned how much hard work, time, and patience it takes to succeed. I've found that each person can make a difference. With the help of my team of "Puffineers," we have succeeded in restoring lost puffin and tern colonies. Too often, people only take things from the earth, but with Project Puffin, we've given something back.

If you decide to visit the Maine coast in the summertime, you may see me out on one of our Audubon islands, where I'm still working to protect and re-establish seabird populations. Tour boats from several different ports make daily trips out to Eastern Egg Rock, Matinicus Rock, and Seal Island. With Audubon naturalists on board to point out sights and sounds, it's a great way to see the birds up close.

The methods we've invented on Maine islands to restore seabird colonies have been used by one of our Audubon teams in the Galapagos Islands, off South America, to help a globally endangered bird called the Dark-rumped Petrel. And biologists in Japan, Hawaii, Canada, and other places are also using our ideas to bring seabird colonies back from the edge of extinction.

But seabirds are just part of the larger picture. Important work is being done all over the world to help wolves, grizzly bears, seals, whales, manatees, gorillas, and many other threatened animals and plants. Many people are involved in protecting and restoring these animals and their habitats as well. And it's not only adults who are doing these things. Young people who care about our beautiful planet are working in their schools, homes, and communities, giving back to the earth.

From the safety of Egg Rock, a group of puffins looks back at the eco-tourists.

Glossary

Billing—When puffins rub their bills together. This strengthens the bond between the male and female.

Burrow—Where a puffin lays its egg. Underground, at the end of a tunnel, or under rocks.

Bird Band—A metal or plastic ring put around a bird's leg for identification. The band has numbers on it and may be colored.

Brooding—When a parent bird keeps a newborn chick warm by nestling it close to its body.

Capelin—A small saltwater fish, eaten by puffins, that can be found in the North Atlantic.

Chick—A very young puffin that is confined to its burrow.

Colony—Many birds of the same kind nesting together.

Decoy—A wooden or plastic bird model.

Eco-tourist—People who travel to see interesting animals, plants and unspoiled scenery.

Fledging—The time when a chick is old enough to leave its nest and live on its own.

Fledgling—What a young bird is called that has left its nest. It is no longer a chick.

Fratercula arctica—The Latin, or scientific name, for the Atlantic Puffin. It means "little brother of the arctic."

Gaping—When a puffin opens its beak to threaten another puffin.

Grubbing—Searching for young seabird chicks, such as puffins, by putting your hands and arms in their underground nesting burrows.

Habitat—Where a particular animal or plant lives. For example, a puffin's habitat is the ocean and the offshore islands it uses to rest on or raise young.

Hake—A saltwater fish eaten by puffins and other seabirds.

Herring—An especially important saltwater fish eaten by puffins and other seabirds.

Incubate—When a parent bird sits on eggs. Heat from the bird's body will slowly cause the eggs to hatch.

Predatory—Describes the behavior of a gull or other meat-eating animal that searches for a live animal to capture and eat.

"Puffineers"—The fun name we call all the people who work on our islands with puffins and other seabirds.

Restore—To bring a species of animal or plant back to a place where it once lived.

Socialize—The ways birds interact with each other.

Wildlife Warden—Someone who protects plants and animals at a park or sanctuary.

Wildlife Sanctuary—Land that is protected to give plants and animals a safe place to live.

Puffin-Watching Boat Trips

The puffin-watching season begins around Memorial Day (the end of May) and ends in early to mid-August. The National Audubon Society places naturalists aboard several different boats to point out wildlife and tell the story of how the puffins and terns came back. Call the boat companies to find out their schedules.

Short Trips

One and one-half hours—from New Harbor, Maine, to Eastern Egg Rock. *Hardy Boat Cruises.* 800-2-PUFFIN.*

Three hours—from Boothbay Harbor, Maine, to Eastern Egg Rock. *Cap'n Fish.* 207-633-3244.*

Long Trips

All Day—from Rockland, Maine, to Matinicus Rock and Seal Island National Wildlife Refuge. *Atlantic Expeditions,* Capt. Bob Bernstein. 207–372–8621.*

All Day—from Jonesport, Maine, to Canadian-owned Machias Seal Island. *Captains John and Barna Norton.* 207-497-5933.

All Day—from Cutler, Maine, to Machias Seal Island. *Bold Coast Charter Company.* 207–259–4484.

*Audubon narrators on board.

Adopt-A-Puffin

You can help support National Audubon Society's Project Puffin by adopting your own puffin! Each $100 gift will enroll you in the Adopt-A-Puffin program and assign one Atlantic Puffin to you. Each puffin was taken on a journey—over 1,000 miles by air, land, and sea—from Newfoundland to grow upon Eastern Egg Rock, off the coast of Maine. Now these puffins are members of the restored community. You will receive your puffin's life story, a full-color photograph of your puffin, and a certificate of adoption.

Many classes and schools have raised money through bake sales, bottle drives, and other methods to adopt a puffin. For more information, write to Project Puffin, National Audubon Society, 159 Sapsucker Woods Road, Ithaca, NY 14850.

Project Puffin Teacher's Guide

Pete Salmansohn and Steve Kress have written a separate activity guide to complement this book. Filled with more than 40 creative, hands-on activities, *Giving Back to the Earth* is organized into seven major themes such as seabird adaptations, the ocean web of life, people making a difference for wildlife, etc. Art projects, role-playing, wildlife observation projects, science demonstrations, running games, and other methods are used to excite and educate youngsters in grades 3 to 6. Original drawings, photographs, and an extensive bibliography accompany the practical and readable text. Published by Tilbury House, 132 Water Street, Gardiner, ME 04345; 800-582-1899.

Saddlestitched, $9.95, ISBN 0-88448-172-7.

To Joe and Mary Johansen,

for twenty years of invaluable logistics, caring, and support to Project Puffin.

Tilbury House, Publishers
132 Water Street
Gardiner, Maine 04345

Library of Congress Cataloging-in-Publication Data:
Kress, Stephen W.
Project Puffin: how we brought puffins back to Egg Rock / by Stephen Kress as told to Pete Salmansohn.
p. cm
"A National Audubon Society Book."
Summary: Details a wildlife scientist's successful efforts to restore puffin colonies in Maine through an experiment in chick translocation.
ISBN 0-88448-170-0
1. Atlantic puffin—Maine—Eastern Egg Rock—Juvenile literature. 2. Wildlife reintroduction—Maine—Eastern Egg Rock—Juvenile literature. [1. Puffins. 2. Wildlife reintroduction. 3. Wildlife conservation.] I. Salmansohn, Pete, 1947– . II. National Audubon Society. III. Title.
QL696.C42K74 1997
636.9'7833—dc29   95-47805
                                                                                        CIP
                                                                                        AC

Photo Credits: All photographs by Stephen Kress except the following:
Page 9 (left), Culver Photos; page 12 (left), by Evie Weinstein; pages 6, 12 (right), 25, 38, 39, 46, Walker Golder; pages 28 and 37(right), Art Gingert; pages 30 and 31, Pete Salmansohn

Text and cover designed by: Susan Sherman, Ars Agassiz, Cambridge, MA
Editing and production: Jennifer Elliott, Mark Melnicove
Sales and promotions: Michelle Gifford
Office: Jolene Collins
Warehouse: William Hoch

Color separations: World Color
Printing and binding: Worzalla, Stevens Point, WI

First edition: March 1997
10 9 8 7 6 5 4 3 2 1